A Note to Parents and

DK READERS is a compelling programme for beginning readers, designed in conjunction with leading literacy experts.

Beautiful illustrations and superb full-colour photographs combine with engaging, easy-to-read stories to offer a fresh approach to each subject in the series. Each DK READER is guaranteed to capture a child's interest while developing his or her reading skills, general knowledge and love of reading.

The five levels of DK READERS are aimed at different reading abilities, enabling you to choose the books that are exactly right for your child:

Pre-level 1 – Learning to read
Level 1 – Beginning to read
Level 2 – Beginning to read alone
Level 3 – Reading alone
Level 4 – Proficient readers

The "normal" age at which a child begins to read can be anywhere from three to eight years old, so these levels are only a general guideline.

No matter which level you select, you can be sure that you are helping your child learn to read, then read to learn!

LONDON, NEW YORK,
MUNICH, MELBOURNE, AND DELHI

Created by Tall Tree Ltd
Editor Jon Richards
Designer Ed Simkins
For DK
Series Editor Alastair Dougall
Series Designer Rob Perry
Editor Laura Gilbert
Production Claire Pearson
DTP/Designer Dean Scholey
Picture Researcher Marie Ortu
Picture Library Kate Ledwith
Cover art by Mike Wieringo and
José Marzan, Jr.

06 07 08 09 10 9 8 7 6 5 4 3

First published in Great Britain in 2005 by Dorling Kindersley
Limited, 80 Strand, London WC2R ORL
A Penguin Company
Page design copyright © 2005 Dorling Kindersley Limited.
FLASH, JLA, and all related characters and elements
are trademarks of DC Comics © 2005. All rights reserved.
No part of this publication
may be reproduced, stored in a retrieval system,
or transmitted in any form or by any means, electronic,
mechanical, photocopying, recording, or otherwise, without
the prior written permission of the copyright owner.

A CIP catalogue record for this book is available from the British Library.

ISBN 1-4053-0430-8

Colour reproduction by Media Development and Printing Ltd, UK
Printed and bound in China by L Rex Printing Co., Ltd.

The publisher would like to thank the following for their kind permission
to reproduce their images:
Position key: c=centre; b=bottom; l=left; r=right; t=top
7 Alamy Images: Ralph Wetmore (t); 8-9 DK Images: NASA (b);
10-11 DK Images: Kenneth Lilly; 14-15 DK Images: Jerry Young;
24-25 DK Images: Chris Grigg/Keither Harmer; 26-27 Rex Features:
Charles M. Ommanney (COY / KMLA); 29 DK Images: Demetrio
Carrasco (b); 30-31 Corbis: Rick Doyle (c); 32-33 DK Images: Richard
Leeney (b); 34-35 DK Images: Richard Leeney (c); 37 DK Images:
NASA (b); 38-39 DK Images: Raymond Turvey; 40-41 Science Photo
Library: Tony & Daphne Hallas (c); 42 DK Images: EADS Astrium (b);
45 Alamy Images: Popperfoto (bl); 47 Rex Features: Novastock (SKC) b.
All other photographs © Dorling Kindersley.
For further information see: www.dkimages.com

**Dorling Kindersley would like to thank the following artists for their
contribution to this book:** Marlo Alquiza, Brian Apthorp, Brandon
Badeaux, Darryl Banks, Hilary Barta, Brian Bolland, Greg Brooks, Joe
Brozowski, Sal Buscema, Jim Calfiore, Sergio Cariello, John Cassaday,
Dave Cockrum, Dan Davis, John Dell, Pamela Eckland, Wayne Faucher,
John Floyd, Kerry Gammill, Brian Garvey, Frank Giacoia, Joe Giella, Dick
Giordano, Doug Hazlewood, Phil Hester, Josh Hood, Carmine Infantino,
Chris Ivy, Dennis Janke, Oscar Jimenez, Phil Jimenez, Gil Kane, Scott
Kolins, Joe Kubert, Greg LaRocque, Jim Lee, Ron Lim, Livesay, Kenny
Martinez, Jose Marzan, Mark McKenna, Jesus Merino, Pop Mhan, Tom
Morgan, Todd Nauck, Carlos Pacheco, Yanick Pacquette, Dan Panosian,
Ande Parks, Bruce Patterson, Paul Pelletier, Andrew Pepoy, Howard
Porter, Mark Prudeau, Humberto Ramos, Roy Richardson, Roger
Robinson, Denis Rodier, Anibal Rodriguez, Vince Russell, Scott Shaw,
Bob Smith, Ray Snyder, Mike Wieringo, Scott Williams, and Pete Woods.

Discover more at
www.dk.com

Contents

DK READERS

PROFICIENT 4 READERS

JLA **THE FLASH'S BOOK OF**

Written by Clare Hibbert

Flash I
Research scientist Jay Garrick was the first-ever Flash. He gained his amazing super-speed after breathing in radioactive fumes.

Flash II
Police chemist Barry Allen, who lived in Central City, was the second Flash. He was also a founding member of the JLA.

Champion speedster

I'm the Flash, also known as the Scarlet Speedster because of my cool costume! There have been different Flashes over the years, but we all share certain things in common. Firstly, of course, we are all capable of superhuman speeds! We gain our power from the Speed Force – a mysterious realm at the far reaches of the Universe. We use our speed for good, helping to fight crime and injustice wherever we find it. That is why we teamed up with other super heroes, such as Batman and Superman, to form the Justice League of America (JLA).

This book is all about the fastest things on planet Earth – and beyond! You'll also find out loads about me, my fellow speedsters, my friends in the JLA, and my enemies.

The most famous Flash was Barry Allen's nephew, Wally West. He became Flash III after Barry's death. He is in the main picture, speeding through the skies.

Flash IV
A new hero took over as the Flash after Wally West disappeared. He turned out to be 27th-century speedster John Fox, who had travelled back in time.

Lightning flash

Sometimes people talk about things happening "as quick as lightning". That is because a bolt of lightning can flash across the sky in a split second.

Thunderstorms are made up of thunder and lightning. They develop inside cumulonimbus clouds. Inside the clouds, raindrops and ice crystals smash into each other, building up positive and negative electrical charges. Electricity flows between the charges, creating a lightning flash that heats the surrounding air until it is five times as hot as the surface of the Sun! The noise that the hot air makes is thunder.

You can work out how far away a thunderstorm is because the light travels faster than sound.

Lightning bolt
Barry Allen became the second Flash after he was struck by a bolt of lightning.

Kid Flash
Wally West was also struck by lightning.
It happened when he was in his uncle's lab – and he became Kid Flash.

Like the Flash, David Hersh the preacher was struck by lightning. He discovered that he could become immortal (live forever) by sacrificing the lives of others, and took the name Cicada.

That means you see the lightning before you hear the thunder, even though they happen at the same time. Count the seconds between the flash and the thunder to find out how far you are from the storm. Divide the number by three to get the distance in kilometres.

The Weather Wizard is one of the Rogues, a band of baddies who hate the Flash. The Weather Wizard uses his Weather Wand to summon up any kind of storm.

Wild winds

The very fastest winds on the planet are found inside a tornado, or twister. Tornadoes are spinning columns of air that reach down from a thundercloud and touch the ground. They spin at speeds of up to 480 km/h (300 mph).

A tornado is like an enormous vacuum cleaner. Its funnel of air sucks up everything in its path, from houses to trains. Tornadoes can happen anywhere in the world, but so many happen in the American Midwest that the area is known as "Tornado Alley". The wind speeds in hurricanes are not as fast as those found in tornadoes.

Even so, these violent tropical storms contain winds that can blow at more than 120 km/h (75 mph). Hurricanes form over warm seas. As the storm races over the water, the winds whip up freak giant waves. These can be big enough to wash away a whole city if the storm hits the coast.

Police work
Like the Flash, Detective Fred Chyre helps to protect Keystone City. He has adopted and raised Josh Jackam, the son of murdered fellow officer Julie. The Weather Wizard recently learned that Josh was actually his son and had inherited some powers of the Weather Wand.

This swirling mass of cloud is a roaring hurricane. The centre of the storm is called the eye.

Fastest animals

The fastest land animal is the sleek-bodied cheetah. It bolts across African grasslands at up to 95 km/h (60 mph). Unlike other cats, the cheetah has blunt, straight claws, like a dog, that cannot be fully retracted (pulled in). These give the cheetah extra grip when it is running down gazelle and other prey. Cheetahs can sprint only for short bursts. The average chase covers just 170 m (183 yd).

Cheetah
Flash's JLA teammate Wonder Woman has battled the ferocious Cheetah. The first Cheetah was Priscilla Rich, a woman who suffered from a split personality after she became jealous of Wonder Woman.

The sailfish can swim even faster than a cheetah runs. It has a powerful body that can propel it through the water at speeds of up to 109 km/h (68 mph). This makes it the fastest creature in the oceans.

However, birds can outpace both land and sea animals. The spine-tailed swift, for instance, can fly at speeds of 170 km/h (106 mph). The fastest animal of all, however, is the peregrine falcon. When this bird of prey swoops down on its target from a great height, it can reach speeds of more than 200 km/h (124 mph), making it the fastest creature on the planet.

Fastback
Timmy Joe Terrapin is from Earth C. Superman, who often raced against the Flash, visited Earth C in a parallel universe. After he was hit by a meteorite, Timmy gained super-speed and became known as Fastback.

The speedy cheetah stalks (closely follows) its prey first, then starts to sprint towards it from about 30 m (100 ft) away.

11

Sporting animals

Watching animals pushing themselves to the limit makes thrilling sport, especially when they achieve high speeds. The best thoroughbred racehorses can gallop along at nearly 70 km/h (43 mph), while the fastest greyhounds – desperate to catch the racetrack's mechanical rabbit – can reach top speeds of just over 65 km/h (40 mph)!

The world's most famous dog-sled race is the yearly Iditarod Trail in Alaska, USA. The record time to complete the 1,800-km (1,120-mile) race is a little over nine days.

Superdog
The special powers of Superman's canine companion, Krypto, include speed, strength, X-ray vision, and the power of flight.

The race celebrates the dog teams that carried life-saving medicine between the towns of Anchorage and Nome. The medicine was needed due to an outbreak of the throat disease diphtheria in 1925.

The sport of racing pigeons began in the 1800s. Races can take place over hundreds or thousands of kilometres, and the bird that covers the distance in the fastest time is the winner. Some racing pigeons can fly at average speeds of more than 145 km/h (90 mph)!

Grodd
The evil Grodd is part of a clan of super-smart gorillas who live in the hidden Gorilla City. He has clashed many times with the Scarlet Speedster.

Dog-sleds are pulled by teams of huskies. With their thick fur and sturdy build, the dogs can cope with extremely low temperatures.

Slow living

Not everything lives at a breakneck speed. The snail is so famous for living life in the slow lane that people even talk about "crawling at a snail's pace". It would take a snail a whole minute just to slither the length of your hand.

The tortoise is also known for its leisurely pace. It does not need to run because its tough, horny shell protects it from harm.

Slow down
As slow as a tortoise, Turtle Man used a ray gun that stole the Flash's powers and gave them to his men. The more the Flash tried to run, the faster the bad guys went.

Planting evil
Poison Ivy can affect how quickly plants grow – and she uses them for her evil plans.

The tree sloth moves very slowly along a jungle branch.

The tree sloth wins the prize for being the laziest animal, snoozing all day and most of the night. It moves so little that algae grows on its hairy body! Even its digestive system is slow – it can take a week to digest a meal.

Of course, plants hardly seem to move at all. The slowest-growing is a fruit tree called the dioon. It grows just 0.77 mm (0.02 inches) in a year.

Chronos
Arch-villain Chronos was able to slow down time, freezing people to the spot. He developed his time-altering powers when he was in prison.

Aquaman is the JLA's best swimmer. He is able to breathe underwater, and he can power along at speeds of up to 160 km/h (100 mph).

Only human
Unlike the other members of the JLA, Batman does not have any superhuman powers. He is simply a human being at the absolute peak of physical fitness.

Human speedsters

Athletes are the closest humans have to speed heroes. The first person to run 1.6 km (1 mile) in less than four minutes was Britain's Roger Bannister in 1954. Since then, speeds have kept improving, thanks to more time spent training and the development of high-performance running shoes. Today's sprinters can top 40 km/h (25 mph) over short distances!

The fastest swimming stroke is the front crawl. The best swimmers can swim at 8 km/h (5 mph) on average.

Surfing is a much faster way to zoom through water, or rather over it, because it harnesses the power of a breaking wave.

Snowboarding is similar to surfing, but faster because the boarders speed across a snowy, slippery hillside. It is still not as popular or as fast as skiing, though. The fastest skiing speeds – achieved over special speed trials – are a mega 240 km/h (150 mph) or more. The best cross-country skiers can only manage average speeds of around 25 km/h (16 mph).

Competitive streak
Whenever Superman and the Flash test their speed against each other, the Flash usually comes out the winner.

Human reactions

Every human being is a champion speedster – on the inside!
The human body is made to react to its changing surroundings faster than the blink of an eye. The brain can trigger movements without us being aware of any thought process.

Icy villain
Captain Cold is one of the few Rogues who can slow down the Flash. The cold-gun he designed creates a "cold field" that halts movement at an atomic level, allowing the fast-moving Flash to be seen.

The quick responses our bodies make to danger are called reflexes. When a nerve ending senses pain, for example, it sends a message to the nearest part of the spinal cord.

At once, a signal travels
back to the body part,
making it jerk away from
the source of the pain.
Doctors can test the
speed of our reflexes by
tapping just below the
kneecap – this should
make the knee jerk!
Nerve cells carry their
speedy signals in the form
of tiny bursts of electricity.
The electricity leaps from
cell to cell along junctions
called synapses in less than
one-thousandth of a second.

Blue baddy
Evil Cobalt
Blue attacked
Sela Allen,
daughter of the
Flash from the
23rd century.
He slowed
down her
nervous system
so that no
messages could
travel from her
brain to her
muscles.
This meant she
was paralysed.

A sprinter cannot leave the blocks until 0.1 seconds after the gun has fired. This is the fastest time it takes for the body to react to the sound of the gun – any quicker and it is a false start.

Fast weapons

In any kind of combat, from one-to-one fighting to full-scale war, a fast weapon gives its owner the edge. People have used bows and arrows for over 30,000 years.

A modern longbow arrow can whizz along at 550 km/h (344 mph).

A cruise missile is a type of weapon that can guide itself to a target.

A *Tomahawk* cruise missile flies through the air at speeds of 880 km/h (550 mph). It is hard to detect because its engine gives off so little heat. The next generation of missiles, planned for 2015, will be even faster, flying at 5,760 km/h (3,600 mph)! That's faster than a speeding bullet – but only just!

Quivering champ
Green Arrow Oliver Queen uses his amazing skill with a bow to save members of the JLA. He fires special, customized arrows, some of which pack a high-explosive punch.

Bulletproof!
Wonder Woman wears bracelets that can deflect bullets. Superman goes one better: bullets bounce off his body without harming him at all.

Depending on its size and shape, a rifle bullet travels at 5,400 km/h (3,375 mph). That means it can cover the length of 13 soccer pitches in less than a second!

21

Terrific two-wheelers

A cycling champ can pedal along at nearly 90 km/h (55 mph) – or even faster if he or she slipstreams behind another vehicle. With lightweight frames and a streamlined shape, today's racing bikes are designed to create less drag and more speed.

The quickest way to travel on two wheels is by motorbike. Racers are the fastest, some topping 300 km/h (186 mph) – as fast as a high-speed train!

Vanishing point
While the Flash was chasing an evil lookalike called the Rival (above), the baddy went faster than the speed of light – and vanished into thin air. He had hit terminal velocity and found the Speed Force!

Scrambling motorbikes are slower, because they're built to take part in tough, cross-country racing.

Motorbike racing is a very popular sport. Speedway racing is for lightweight motorbikes on a racetrack. The most famous speedway event is held each March at Daytona, Florida, USA.

Long-distance speedsters prefer the gruelling Paris-Dakar rally, a 11,265-km (7,000-mile) race that is open to cars and trucks as well as bikes. Part of the course is through very hot desert, so it's no wonder that competitors try to finish the race as quickly as possible!

Power source
The Speed Force is an energy field that exists beyond the speed of light. Max Mercury (above), the Flash's friend, discovered that all speedsters drew their powers from this mysterious energy field.

Four wheels

Dark Knight's charger
With its lightweight metal frame and 1,500-horsepower engine, the Batmobile has a cruising speed of 360 km/h (225 mph). It can even reach 565 km/h (350 mph) for short bursts, thanks to its powerful jet afterburner.

Car racing has been a sport almost since the invention of the engine. The first big car race, or Grand Prix, took place in 1895 in France, when the winning car averaged a speed of about 24 km/h (15 mph)!

Modern racing cars are quite a bit faster than that!

Formula One Grand Prix racing cars are only allowed small engines, but they can still reach speeds of more than 260 km/h (160 mph). In other races, such as the Daytona Busch Clash, normal cars are "souped up" and raced at speeds of 320 km/h (200 mph).

24

Dragsters are the fastest wheel-driven cars of all. They have huge engines on tiny, slender frames, with small wheels at the front and huge tyres at the back. The huge rear tyres give the dragsters as much grip as possible. Dragsters are raced on a straight strip and they can zoom to speeds of over 500 km/h (300 mph). They even have to use parachutes to slow them to a halt!

Overtaking
After he was struck by lightning, Barry Allen wasn't aware of his new powers at first. The first he knew was when he ran for a taxi – and overtook it!

Some dragsters increase their speed so quickly that they have a bar at the back to stop them from flipping over.

Super cars

Rogue machine
Young Tony Gambi agreed to help the Rogues defeat the new Flash. They put him inside a machine called the Humanifold in order to create a super rogue.

To go faster than a dragster, a vehicle has to be very streamlined to cut through the air surrounding its body. Record breakers have to use rockets or jet engines. *The Blue Flame* was a rocket-powered car that reached 1,016 km/h (635 mph) in 1970.

Travelling at close to the speed of sound in a car is risky. The ground has to be smooth, since the slightest bump could flip the car and destroy it – and its driver.

Thrust SSC *roars across the desert to set a new land-speed record.*

Land-speed record breakers use natural flat surfaces, such as the Bonneville Salt Flats, Utah, USA, to race their machines against the clock.

Jet-propelled cars are the fastest cars in the world. The land-speed record was set in a car called *Thrust SSC*, which used two supersonic-fighter jet engines to generate around 110,000 horsepower! It was the first car to travel faster than the speed of sound, setting a speed record of 1,228 km/h (768 mph) in 1997.

Transformation
Record breakers add jet engines to improve their cars. The Humanifold bonded the Rogues' weapons to Tony's body, creating the Ultimate Rogue. They called him Replicant!

Fast track

Trains have always been symbols of rapid scientific progress. The first trains reached speeds of 40 km/h (25 mph), which some people believed would be too fast for the human body to survive! Modern high-speed trains reach ten times that speed, perfectly safely. The fastest train is the French TGV – "TGV" stands for the French words *Train à Grand Vitesse*, meaning "High-Speed Train". The TGV reached an incredible 515 km/h (322 mph) in special test runs in 1990, though it normally works at about 240 km/h (150 mph). The Japanese Bullet Train's normal speed is even greater, averaging speeds of 273 km/h (171 mph).

Hometown
Apart from being home to the Flash, Keystone City is famous for its speedy train network. It is linked to Central City by a huge iron and steel bridge. The Flash assembled the bridge after a villain called Blacksmith demolished the old one.

The Japanese rail service is testing a new train. It has reached speeds of 552 km/h (345 mph). Seconds after leaving the station, the train's wheels retract, and the train "flies" above the track on a cushion of magnetic fields.

Tornado Twins Born in the 30th century, Dawn and Donald Allen inherited speed from their father, Barry Allen. They fought crime in secret, disguised as tornadoes!

The Japanese Bullet Train's curved nose is based on the streamlined shape of an aircraft.

Water speedsters

When he wants to swim even faster, Aquaman hitches a ride on the back of a killer whale.

Speed through the water is measured in knots, from an old technique for measuring a ship's speed by feeding out a rope with knots tied in it. Knots measure speed across nautical miles, and one knot equals 1.85 km/h (1.15 mph).

It's hard to be speedy over water. Water is thicker and heavier than air, so it drags on vessels and slows things down.

Walking on water
Crossing a body of water holds no problems for the Scarlet Speedster. He runs so fast that he can just zip across the surface.

The fastest water craft contact the water as little as possible. The *Decavitator* is a strange water speedster – it has no engine! It uses an air propeller, powered by a "cyclist" in a streamlined cockpit. In 1991 it reached a speed of 18.5 knots, or 34 km/h (21 mph). Motorized water racers can go much faster – a water bike can manage 56 knots, or 104 km/h (65 mph). Hydroplanes are fastest of all because they skip along the surface of the water. In 1978, a hydroplane called the *Spirit of Australia* reached a record-breaking speed of 276 knots, or 511 km/h (317 mph).

Johnny Quick
Crime-fighter Johnny Quick knows a secret formula that connects him to the Speed Force. It is based on a sacred mantra found inside the tomb of an Egyptian pharaoh.

Johnny Quick was an All-Star Squadron hero during World War II.

High fliers

The fastest record breakers break away from the surface of the Earth. Many jet planes break the sound barrier, which means they travel faster than the speed of sound. At ground level, the sound barrier lies at 1,216 km/h (760 mph). High above the Earth, where the air is thinner, the sound barrier is broken at 1,040 km/h (650 mph).

When a vehicle breaks the sound barrier, it travels faster than its own noise. Noise piles up behind it to form a shockwave, which is heard on the ground as a bang, or "sonic boom".

The first aircraft to break the sound barrier was a Bell X-1, flown by Chuck Yeager in 1947.

Quick flight
Although she cannot achieve the speeds of the Flash, Jesse Quick has mastered how to go fast enough to take off!

The X-series of aircraft have been record breakers ever since. An unmanned X-43A aircraft broke all records in 2004. It reached a speed seven times faster than the speed of sound, at 7,648 km/h (4,780 mph).

Ring of light
Green Lantern's ring can shape light into solid forms instantly, creating anything that the wearer imagines, such as a protective shield.

This is one of three X-1 supersonic planes built in the 1940s. The "X" stood for "experimental".

Jets and rockets

Jet engines struggle to "breathe" at the highest speeds. It is easier to use rocket engines to push beyond the records achieved by the X-43A. Rockets do not have to collect oxygen from the air they are travelling through to burn their fuel – everything they need for thrust is carried in tanks.

The US X-15 rocket plane was lifted to a high altitude (height) by an enormous B-52 bomber. Once there, it dropped off the bomber's wing and fired up its own rocket engine. This took it so high and fast that its test pilots were counted as "astronauts" by the US Air Force!

Sonic boom
The Pied Piper used special sonic (sound) weapons against the Flash. Like his namesake, he also enchanted people with his flute-playing.

NASA

6667

H₂O₂ JETT

34

One of them, Neil Armstrong, later joined NASA and became the first man to walk on the Moon. The X-15 reached 7,322 km/h (4,520 mph). Only space rockets have ever carried human beings faster than this.

The X-15 flew at nearly seven times the speed of sound!

Racy robots
In the 27th century, a breed of speedy robots was developed to serve with the police force. The Speed Metal robots help the new Flash to track down criminals.

The Speed Metal robots are fitted with time-travelling devices so that they can track and chase criminals through time.

Blastoff!

You have to go pretty fast to escape the pull of Earth's gravity. The speed needed to overcome gravity and escape into outer space is called "escape velocity". From Earth, escape velocity is about 40,200 km/h (25,000 mph).

The US space agency NASA built the gigantic Saturn V rockets to push Moon missions clear of the Earth. Each rocket stood 111 m (364 ft) tall, and weighed nearly 3,000 tonnes (3 million kg). Most of this weight was the fuel needed to power the rocket.

Earth's atmosphere is thin near space, but there are still enough gas particles to create heat through friction. Anything moving through air at high speed heats up. When astronauts return to Earth, they hit the atmosphere at nearly 32,000 km/h (20,000 mph).

All change
The Flash's costume can withstand the heat produced by high-speed travel and its outer layer of Teflon minimizes air resistance!

The Flash's costume fits inside a custom-built ring. When the ring is released, gases in the air expand the suit so that it can expand to full size.

Air friction acts as a brake to slow the craft down. The underside of the spacecraft is coated with high-tech fireproofing materials – so it does not burn up like a shooting star.

Rocket boots
Honorary JLA member Steel cannot fly – but he does have a pair of jet boots! These allow him to rocket up into the air.

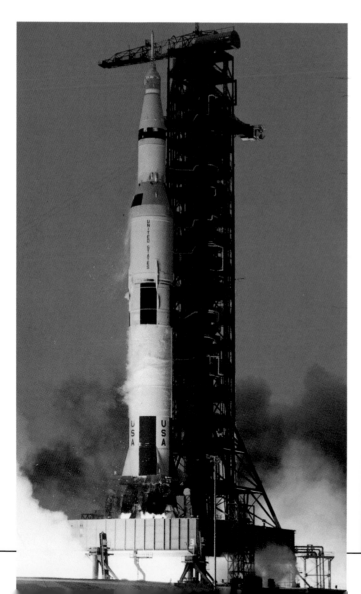

The Saturn V rocket blasts clear of the launchpad. It was the largest rocket NASA ever used and carried people to the Moon and the Skylab space station into orbit in the 1960s and 1970s.

Speed in space

JLA satellite
For a while, the Justice League of America's headquarters was a satellite in orbit above the Earth. Later, the League built the Watchtower on the Moon.

Speed in space is hard to measure, because everything is moving – there is no fixed point to measure against. By using the Sun as a point to measure from, however, we know that the planets of the Solar System loop around the Sun at incredible speeds.

The Earth's orbit around the Sun takes precisely one year – that's what a year measures! Each second, the Earth moves nearly 30 km (19 miles).

That's a speed of 107,283 km/h (67,052 mph)!

Some of the other planets of the Solar System are even faster. Mercury, tucked in close to the surface of the Sun, zooms around it in a circuit at nearly 172,800 km/h (108,000 mph). Mercury's orbit takes just 88 Earth-days to complete, compared to Earth's 365.

Distant Pluto plods along at a mere 17,280 km/h (10,800 mph), and takes nearly 250 years to complete one lap around the Sun.

Green man
J'onn J'onzz, the Martian Manhunter, is one of the most committed members of the JLA. His special powers include telepathy (being able to read people's minds), shape-shifting, and the ability to reach great speeds.

The Martian Manhunter can also fly and has the ability to make himself intangible so that objects pass right through him!

Black Flash
The Black
Flash is the
form that
Death takes
when it comes
for speedsters.
It was seen
before the
deaths of
Barry Allen and
Johnny Quick.

Distant speedsters

Even the Sun, known in astronomy as Sol, is speeding along. It is moving in a huge circuit around the centre of our galaxy, the Milky Way. Astronomers think this lap takes Sol about 226 million years to complete. That might seem lazy, but only because it is such an enormous distance to travel – the Sun is zooming along at about 777,600 km/h (486,000 mph)!

Galaxies move, too. The nearest galaxy to the Milky Way is called Andromeda. It is too far away to measure the distance in kilometres or miles. Instead, we use light-years – the distance a beam of light can travel in one year.

Andromeda is 2.2 million light-years from the Milky Way. However, we are approaching it at a speed of about 500,000 km/h (312,500 mph). At this rate, the two galaxies will collide in 3,500 million years.

The Andromeda galaxy is the most distant object you can see with the naked eye.

Zippy data

The speed of light is used to measure the big distances of deep space because it is the fastest thing known to science. Light travels at about 300,000 km (186,500 miles) per second, or 1,000 million km/h (625 million mph).

Brain drain

The spare space in the Flash's brain was taken over by an alien probe from the giant starfish-shaped alien Starro (above). Batman freed Wally West from Starro's clutches, and the Flash speedily destroyed the evil alien's computer.

This soldier's field telephone transmits data by satellite dish.

People use light speeds to transfer data around the world. We can send a beam of light along an optical fibre, and use a detector at the other end to decode the signal very rapidly.

Light speed applies to many types of energy rays, not just the light waves that are visible to human eyes. The radio signals that bounce via a satellite around the curve of the Earth are also travelling at light speed.

Electrons inside computers and ordinary wire cables travel slightly slower than light. However, even these signals are far quicker than the messages that flash along our nerves and through our bodies.

Bat computer
In the shadows of the Batcave sits the most advanced computer in the world. It provides Batman with all the information he needs to fight crime.

Strange forces

The speed of light has a special place in the way that science understands the Universe. It appears in the most famous physics equation of all time, $E=mc^2$, part of Albert Einstein's Theory of Relativity. The "E" in this equation stands for energy, "m" for mass, and "c" for the speed of light.

Light always travels at a certain speed in space. This is a breath-taking 1,000 million km/h (625 million mph). This knowledge gives scientists useful clues to the basic rules of physics. It is also handy for astronomers, helping them to understand what they see through their telescopes.

Einstein's theory also shows how space, time, and gravity make up one fabric, obeying clear mathematical rules.

For normal objects, the faster they travel, the more energy they need to accelerate. This makes it impossible for anything other than energy rays to travel at the speed of light.

German-American physicist Albert Einstein lived from 1879 to 1955. In 1921, he was awarded the Nobel Prize for Physics.

Stealing time
Evil scientist T.O. Morrow invented a fourth-dimensional grapple machine to steal inventions from the future.

Good vibrations
The Flash is able to vibrate so fast that he can move through solid objects.

The Cosmic Treadmill

Barry Allen developed a treadmill that could launch him back or forward in time, when he ran on it at top speed. The Cosmic Treadmill also allowed him to reach parallel universes.

After Barry's death, the Cosmic Treadmill became an exhibit in Keystone's famous Flash Museum.

Beyond light speed?

Even travelling at the speed of light, reaching other stars would take tens or even thousands of years. So there are good reasons to look for quicker ways to travel.

Some scientists are looking into particles that can travel faster than light. These imagined particles are called tachyons. We are a long way from creating tachyon spaceships, however. First, we need to invent experiments to test whether tachyons even exist.

Another possibility is that we might discover shortcuts through space, or wormholes. If they existed, wormholes would be very small and exist for only a fraction of a second. We would need to discover how to make them bigger and last longer.

A third idea could be to bend or "warp" space, bringing distant points closer together. This is

how some spaceships travel in movies. Warp engines might be possible in theory, but they would need more fuel than exists in the whole Universe!

Professor Zoom
The Reverse-Flash used the Cosmic Treadmill to time-travel into the past and fight the Flash.

Space is so huge that travelling to other stars, similar to our Sun, would take millions of years using the rockets we have today.